The First Christmas

SOPHIA
INSTITUTE PRESS

Text Copyright © 2019 Thomas D. Williams
Images Copyright © 2019 Frank Fraser

Printed in the United States of America.

Sophia Institute Press®
Box 5284, Manchester, NH 03108
1-800-888-9344

www.SophiaInstitute.com

Sophia Institute Press® is a registered trademark of Sophia Institute.

Library of Congress Control Number:2019948911

The First CHRISTMAS

Thomas D. Williams
ILLUSTRATED BY FRANK FRASER

SOPHIA INSTITUTE PRESS
Manchester, NH

Long, long ago in a
Land we call holy
Was born a great King
In a manner most lowly.

The King's name was Jesus;
His mother was Mary.
To neighbors and friends
It seemed quite ordinary.

But this birth was different: it had been foretold
By sages and prophets and seers of old.
A virgin would bring forth a child, said Isaiah.
From Egypt the boy would emerge, wrote Hosea.

An angel to Mary proclaimed with a nod,
"Hail thee, full of grace, you've found favor with God!"
A maid was this Mary, no more than sixteen.
She puzzled at what this strange greeting could mean.

The angel continued revealing God's plan:
She would be a mother while knowing no man.
"The power of God will enfold you, fair one,
And thus your sweet child will be known as God's Son."

And Mary replied to the message she heard,
"Be it done unto me as announced by your word.
I am but the handmaid of God," she confessed,
"Yet all generations will hence call me blest."

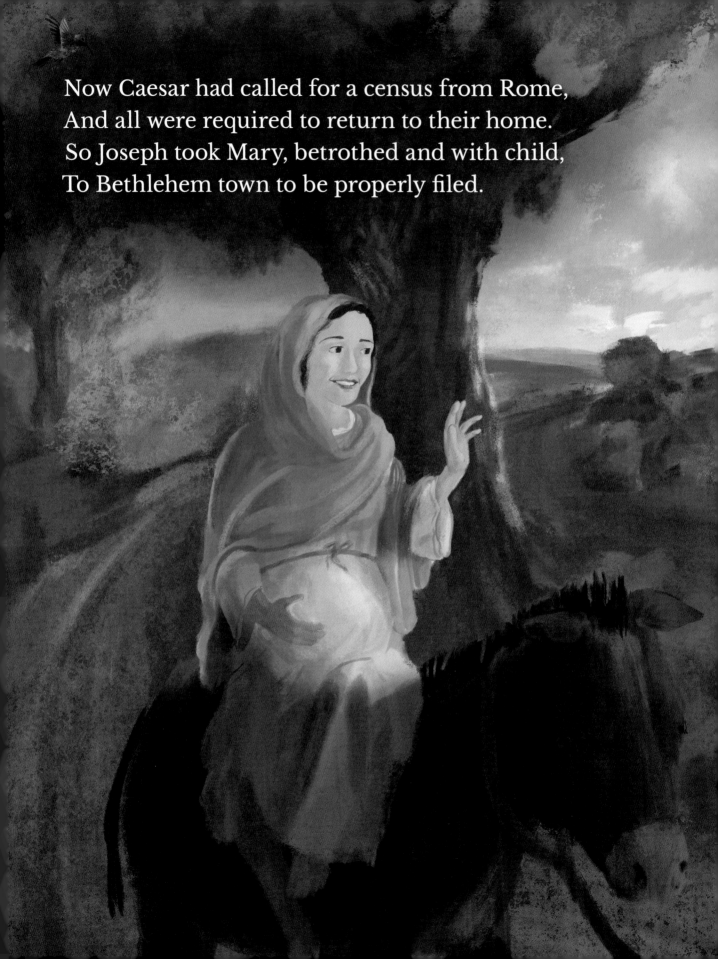

Now Caesar had called for a census from Rome,
And all were required to return to their home.
So Joseph took Mary, betrothed and with child,
To Bethlehem town to be properly filed.

Arriving at last, Joseph learned with chagrin,
There was for his family no room at the inn.
The only choice now was to lodge in a stable,
And take care of Mary as best he was able.

So Jesus the Savior was born in such straits,
With no trumpet fare or festoons on the gates.
Swaddled in blankets and laid in a manger,
The Christ Child came unto his own as a stranger.

Yet shepherds nearby who were tending their herds
Were greeted with splendor and angelic words.
"Fear not," spoke the host, "we bear news of great joy:
The Lord, mighty God, has become a small boy."

The herdsmen went down and found Christ with his mother
And smiled and rejoiced and embraced one another.
"He came down to save us," they said with delight,
"And all future peoples will speak of this night."

Both awed and amazed, they returned to their flocks,
First bidding farewell to the ass and the ox.
To all on their path they proclaimed the great news:
"In Bethlehem town's born the *King of the Jews!*"

And then from the East came three men pure and wise.
They'd seen his star's birth as they searched through the skies.
With gold, myrrh, and incense to gift him, they bowed —
An act quite unknown to the haughty and proud.

As princes and powers in ignorance slept,
The Virgin's heart tending these mysteries kept.
For on that still night, the world shifted its course,
A babe in a manger its unlikely source.

Yet nothing thenceforth
Has e'er been quite the same.
No redemption, no heaven,
Apart from that name.

So this is the reason
We wish well and right,

"Merry Christmas to all,
And to all a good night!"

The End.